A-10 THUNDERBOLTS

BY DEREK ZOBEL

BELLWETHER MEDIA · MINNEAPOLIS, MN

Are you ready to take it to the extreme?
Torque books thrust you into the action-packed
world of sports, vehicles, and adventure. These books
may include dirt, smoke, fire, and dangerous stunts.
WARNING: read at your own risk.

Library of Congress Cataloging-in-Publication Data

Zobel, Derek, 1983-
  A-10 Thunderbolts / by Derek Zobel.
     p. cm. — (Torque: military machines)
  Includes bibliographical references and index.
  Summary: "Amazing photography and engaging information explain the technologies and
capabilities of the A-10 Thunderbolts. Intended for students in grades 3 through 7"—Provided by
publisher.
  ISBN-13: 978-1-60014-201-7 (hardcover : alk. paper)
  ISBN-10: 1-60014-201-X (hardcover : alk. paper)
  1. A-10 (Jet attack plane)—Juvenile literature. 2. Airplanes, Military—United States—Juvenile
literature. I. Title.

  UG1242.A28Z63 2008
  623.74'63—dc22   2008019861

This edition first published in 2009 by Bellwether Media.

The photographs in this book are reproduced through the courtesy of the United States Department of
Defense.

Printed in the United States of America.

CONTENTS

★ ★ ★

THE A-10 THUNDERBOLT IN ACTION

Ground troops are involved in a large battle. An enemy tank is blocking the road. The commander calls on the radio for **close air support**. An A-10 Thunderbolt takes off toward the battle.

The A-10 Thunderbolt is sometimes called the "Warthog" because of its ugly appearance.

The A-10 pilot spots the roadblock ahead and opens fire with the A-10's **GAU-8/A Avenger Gatling gun**. Troops scatter, but the tank is not damaged. The A-10 cruises over the tank and drops two bombs. Now the road is clear. The ground troops can pass safely.

TANKBUSTER

The A-10 Thunderbolt supports ground forces in battle. It carries out attacks against enemy bases, as well as tanks and other armored vehicles. During war, the United States Air Force keeps A-10s at bases near the front line of battle. That way, the planes can help the ground troops wherever they are needed. The most common target of the A-10 is tanks. That is why the plane is sometimes called the "tankbuster."

★ **FAST FACT** ★

Each A-10 Thunderbolt costs $9.8 million.

Compared to other jet planes, the A-10 is not a fast aircraft. Its top speed is only 420 miles (676 kilometers) per hour. However, its slow speed allows for great **maneuverability**. The A-10 can maneuver around a battlefield and attack several targets.

WEAPONS AND FEATURES

The A-10 is heavily armed for battle. Its main weapon is the GAU-8/A Avenger Gatling gun. It can fire 3,900 rounds per minute. That's 65 rounds per second! The GAU-8/A can destroy a wide variety of targets, including tanks.

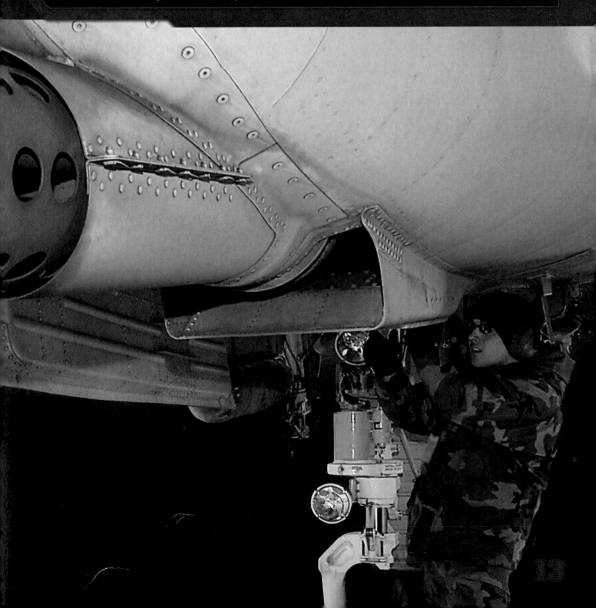

★ **FAST FACT** ★

The Air Force built the A-10 Thunderbolt to replace another powerful plane, the P-47 Thunderbolt.

Thunderbolt pilots use other weapons as well. One type is the **cluster bomb**. These bombs contain hundreds of smaller bombs that can destroy targets over a wide area. Pilots drop bombs on enemy **fortifications**. They may also shoot rockets at tanks and other ground vehicles. Missiles can destroy enemy aircraft.

A-10 THUNDERBOLT SPECIFICATIONS:

Primary Function: Close air support, Forward air control

Length: 53 feet, 4 inches (16.16 meters)

Height: 14 feet, 8 inches (4.42 meters)

Weight: 29,000 pounds (13,154 kilograms)

Wingspan: 57 feet, 6 inches (17.42 meters)

Speed: 420 miles (676 kilometers) per hour

Range: 800 miles (1,287 kilometers)

A-10 MISSIONS

A-10s can have two different missions during battle. They provide close air support and **forward air control**. Close air support means that they are at a base near the battlefield and can fly in to help ground troops. Forward air control means that A-10s guide other aircraft in assaults on ground targets.

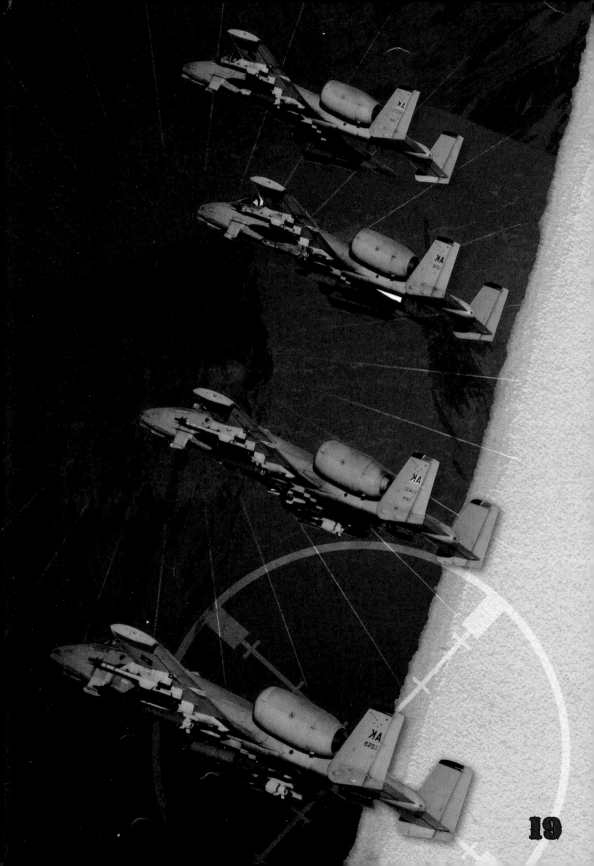

Both of these roles put the A-10 on the front lines. The planes are in constant danger from enemy fire and are therefore made to be very **durable**. The A-10 can lose an engine, a tail fin, or half a wing, and still remain in the air. Because of this, A-10s are sometimes called the tanks of the air.

GLOSSARY

close air support—the role of supporting and protecting ground troops against enemy forces; close air support is a common mission of the A-10.

cluster bomb—a bomb that contains several smaller bombs; cluster bombs hit a wider area than standard bombs.

durable—strong and long-lasting

fortifications—structures built to strengthen a military position

forward air control—the role of guiding other aircraft against enemy targets on the ground; forward air control is a common mission of the A-10.

GAU-8/A Avenger Gatling gun—the main gun of the A-10

maneuverability—an aircraft's ability to change direction and speed

TO LEARN MORE

AT THE LIBRARY

Green, Michael and Gladys. *Close Air Support Fighters: The A-10 Thunderbolt IIs.* Minneapolis, Minn.: Capstone, 2003.

Stone, Lynn M. *A-10 Thunderbolt II.* Vero Beach, Fla.: Rourke, 2004.

Zobel, Derek. *United States Air Force.* Minneapolis, Minn.: Bellwether, 2008.

ON THE WEB

Learning more about military machines is as easy as 1, 2, 3.

1. Go to www.factsurfer.com

2. Enter "military machines" into search box.

3. Click the "Surf" button and you will see a list of related web sites.

With factsurfer.com, finding more information is just a click away.

INDEX